The Fabulous Story of
Fashion

Katie Daynes

Illustrated by Nilesh Mistry

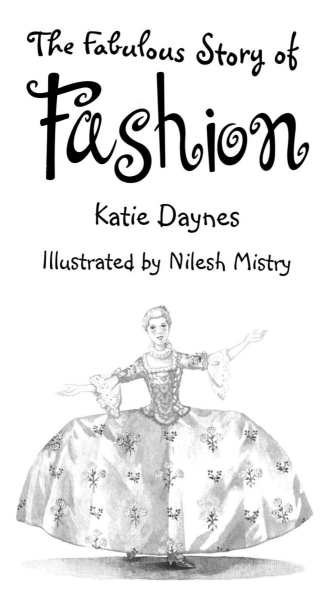

Fashion expert: Cally Blackman

Reading consultant: Alison Kelly
Roehampton University

Contents

Chapter 1

What to wear

Clothes have been worn ever since an early hunter shivered in the cold. He looked enviously at the wild boar he was chasing and thought, "I want that coat."

Throughout history, people in the same area have tended to dress the same way. But local leaders wanted to stand out in a crowd.

Native American chiefs were the men wearing the most feathers.

Viking chiefs had the biggest armlets.

Successful leaders had money and power – and they wore extravagant outfits to prove it. They were the fashion setters of their times.

As for ordinary people, they just admired from a distance.

5

Chapter 2

The Ancient World

The Ancient Egyptians really knew how to dress. Pharaohs, queens and high priests draped themselves in fine, light linen. Some high priests wore panther skins too.

6

On grand occasions, important men and women wore thick wigs and heavy eyeliner. Their arms jangled with chunky gold and silver bracelets, and around their necks they hung ornate collars, threaded with jewels and beads.

Meanwhile, powerful warriors were setting the trends in Ancient Greece.

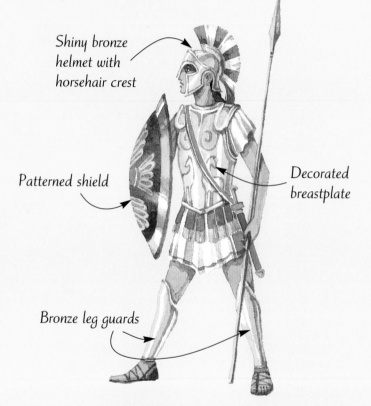

Shiny bronze helmet with horsehair crest

Patterned shield

Decorated breastplate

Bronze leg guards

Their outfits didn't just protect them in battle, they also impressed everyone around them.

In Ancient Rome, the richer you were, the more fabric you wore. Everyone went around in a short dress called a tunic, but important Romans wore togas too.

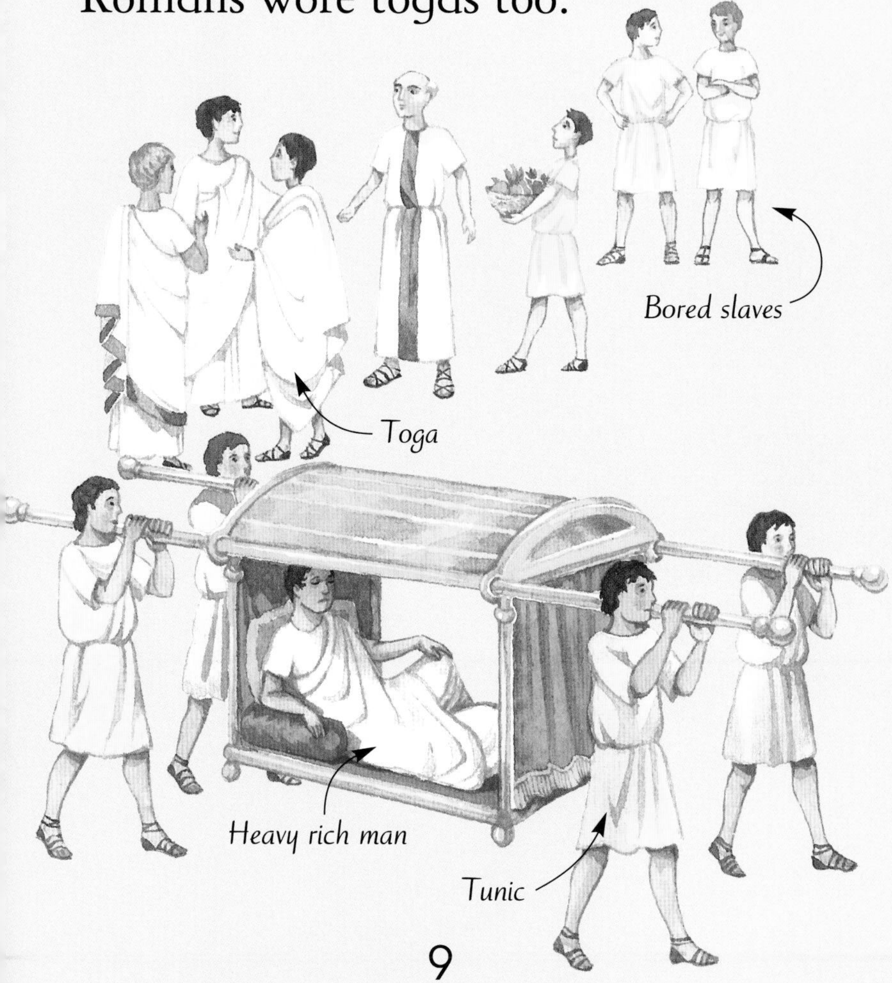

Bored slaves

Toga

Heavy rich man

Tunic

9

Togas were like a semi-circular blanket. A Roman draped one end over his left shoulder...

...and brought the other end around under his right arm.

Then he flung the right end over his left shoulder...

...and tucked the middle piece into his belt.

10

Roman women wore elegant long dresses and shawls. The most fashionable fabrics were brightly dyed cottons or silks.

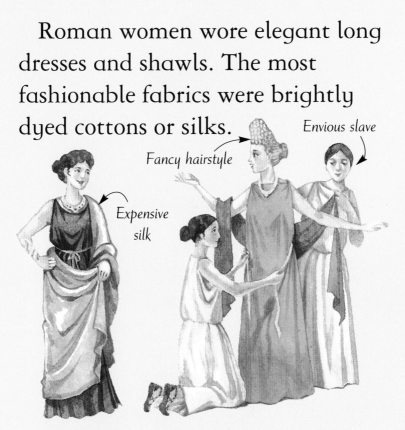

Fancy hairstyle

Envious slave

Expensive silk

Of all the dyes, purple was the rarest and most expensive. Only the emperor could dress entirely in purple. As for silk, it came all the way from China and was worth its weight in gold.

Trade and travel had a big influence on fashion. The wealthy Byzantine emperors bought cotton from the South, jewels and silks from the East and fur from the North.

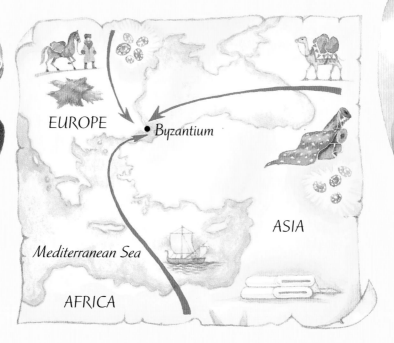

EUROPE

• Byzantium

ASIA

Mediterranean Sea

AFRICA

Emperor Justinian and his wife, Theodora, loved silk, but they resented paying so much for it.

"If only we could make our own..." they thought. But only the Chinese knew how to make silk. Then Justinian persuaded two monks to share the secret...

Silk comes from silkworms.

They spin a silk cocoon around themselves...

...before turning into moths.

The Chinese unravel silk from the cocoons and use it themselves.

For a large fee, the monks went back to China, hid some silkworm eggs in a hollow cane and smuggled them into Byzantium.

Soon, the Byzantine silk industry was booming and their fashions were more lavish than ever. Leading the way was Empress Theodora, dressed in shimmering silk, a sparkling crown and strings of gleaming pearls.

Chapter 3

Knights and maidens

For hundreds of years, silk only reached the kings and queens of Europe. Most lords and ladies swept around their castles in long wool dresses, often lined with fur for extra warmth.

Then Crusader knights returned from battles in the East. They brought with them exotic fabrics and fashions. Soon everyone wanted to wear richly embroidered designs, but still only the wealthy could afford them.

A Crusader knight

A horned headdress

Ladies in the castles would spend hours getting dressed. They liked to coil their hair and wear extravagant headdresses.

A butterfly veil

A steeple headdress

Knights also dressed to impress. They had hearts to win as well as battles.

When a fair maiden fell for a gallant knight, she gave him her handkerchief or glove for luck. He would proudly tie it to his helmet and gallop into battle.

Chapter 4

Flattering fashions

By the 1400s, people decided there was more to fashion than rich fabrics. They wanted their clothes to be flattering too. Women's dresses became low-cut with narrow waists, wide skirts and close-fitting sleeves.

Rich ladies often wore a sideless,
fur-lined gown over the top. It
allowed glimpses of the
fitted dress below.

On colder days they
wore fuller gowns
of thick velvet to
keep out the
castle drafts.

Noblemen now wore short gowns
that opened at the front, revealing
their trendy *doublet and hose*.
The doublet was a short,
decorated tunic, while
the silky hose were
like fancy leggings.

Doublet

Hose

Codpiece

Proudly laced onto the front of
their hose was a *codpiece* – a small
bag where gentlemen stuffed their
money and handkerchief.

21

These fashions were first seen in the Italian and Spanish courts, but they rapidly spread over Europe. Royal dances turned into fashion parades, with people competing to be the best-dressed guest.

Kings and queens worried that their subjects were dressing better than them. "Their clothes should reflect their place in society," they decided.

So they introduced laws on who could wear what.

Philippe le Bel of France ruled that only members of the royal household could wear the finest furs.

Edward III of England set limits on how long men's shoes could be.

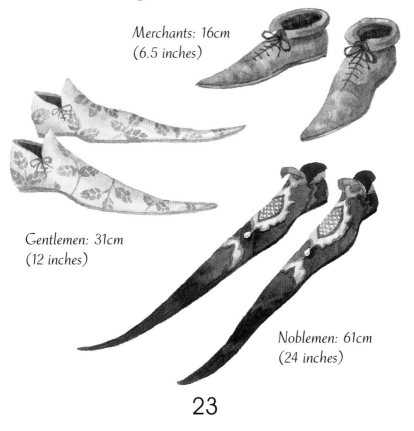

Merchants: 16cm
(6.5 inches)

Gentlemen: 31cm
(12 inches)

Noblemen: 61cm
(24 inches)

And rulers in Italy banned ladies from wearing expensive gold or silver cloth. But people found sneaky ways around these laws. Italian ladies sewed gold or silver linings inside their dresses, then slashed their sleeves so the shiny cloth peeked through.

Within months, slashed sleeves were all the rage.

Chapter 5

Tudor trends

The Tudor king, Henry VIII, took English fashion to new heights. He loved displaying his power and wealth by dressing in sumptuous clothes, dripping with jewels.

During his reign, men's clothing
was more extravagant than women's.
Men wore five basic garments:

Doublet

Linen shirt

Hose

Sleeveless
jerkin

Knee-length gown

Padded shoulders and heavy
fabrics created a bulky, male look.
King Henry topped his outfit
with a fancy hat,
pinned with jewels
and trimmed
with ostrich
feathers.

Slashed
doublet

Fur-lined gown,
embroidered with gold

Full-skirted
jerkin

When his daughter, Elizabeth,
came to the throne, she introduced
even brighter clothes and a passion
for embroidery.

Embroidery was part of every woman's education. It added interest to any garment and it also contained hidden messages.

Serpents were seen as a symbol of wisdom...

...while ears and eyes suggested knowledge.

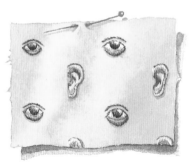

Queen Elizabeth asked for all three symbols on her new outfits.

She commissioned portraits of herself, in her most impressive clothes, and hung them up around her kingdom.

During Elizabeth's reign, an exciting new fashion accessory arrived from Spain. It was a hooped framework, known as a *farthingale*. Soon every woman wanted one under her dress.

Shaped like a bell, the farthingale made skirts flare out and exaggerated women's tiny waists.

It was also the perfect way to hide a pregnancy. Ladies could still attend royal parties, without letting on they were expecting a baby.

Another Spanish import was the popular lacy *ruff*. It started life as a shirt collar. But collars became so frilly, it was much easier to make them separately. Women and men simply tied these ruffs around their necks.

Children wore lacy ruffs too, along with mini versions of all their parents' clothes. But toddlers had their own dress code. Little boys and girls looked exactly the same, wearing a dress, an apron, a bib and a cap.

A boy

A girl

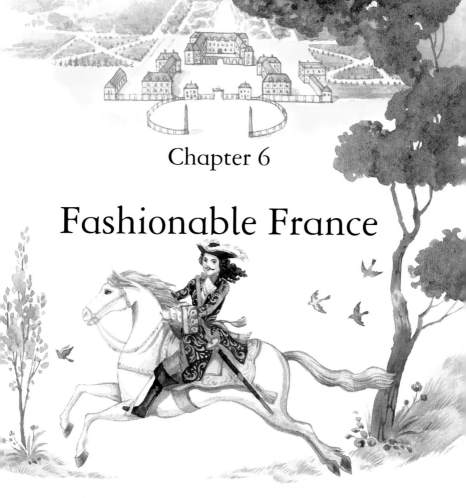

Chapter 6

Fashionable France

By the 17th century, France was
dominating European fashion.
King Louis XIV rode around
wearing a knee-length jacket over
a knee-length waistcoat.

On his head he wore a long, curly wig. His courtiers were quick to copy him. The finest wigs, made of human hair, were a status symbol for the rich. Poorer men made do with goats' hair, horse hair or wool.

Human hair

Goats' hair

Wool

Clothes were made to fit exactly. This forced noblemen and women to slow down and move gracefully. If a man sat down too quickly, his tight hose would split.

So he slid one foot in front of the other...

placed his hands on the arms of a chair...

...and gently lowered himself onto the seat.

Women's movements were even more restricted. They wore two layers of tops, known as *bodies* or *bodices*. With strips of whalebone sewn into their seams, the bodices were designed to flatten women's stomachs. They were laced so tightly, even breathing was hard.

Louis XIV wanted other countries to know that French fashions were best. So he ordered his servants to send large dolls, dressed in the latest styles, to every court in Europe.

Noble ladies cooed over the fabulous designs. "Copy that dress!" they told their tailors.

The tailors would painstakingly unpick the outfits, to see exactly how they'd been made.

French ladies looked at royalty for new dress ideas. During Louis XV's reign, it was his mistress, Madame de Pompadour, who was queen of fashion.

She had a hairstyle named after her...

The Pompadour coiffure

several fabrics...

Pompadour silk

...and even a style of shoe.

The Pompadour heel

Hot on her trail was the Austrian archduchess, Marie Antoinette. She married Louis's grandson and became Queen of France.

Her extravagant clothes were designed by Rose Bertin, the first fashion designer to be known by name. Bertin specialized in elegant silk gowns, embellished with flowers, ribbons and pretty lace.

Her creations were shown off in the world's first fashion magazines. These were thin journals, issued every other week, filled with detailed descriptions and illustrations.

They allowed fashion enthusiasts to keep up-to-date with the trends, without needing to hunt down the latest fashion doll.

At court, people decided dress hoops were a sign of wealth. The wider the hoops, the wealthier the wearer. Very rich women had to turn sideways just to enter a room.

Many palaces had their doorways widened to avoid embarrassment.

After the French revolution, Napoleon came to power. He realized that France's fashions could make his country rich. "We must only buy French lace," he ordered. "And women must wear a different dress each time they come to court."

Meanwhile, the styles became simpler and more graceful, inspired by Ancient Greece and Rome.

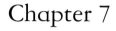

Chapter 7

Fashion for all

Keeping up with the latest trends was expensive. Not only were the fabrics costly, you also had to pay a tailor to sew each item by hand.

By the 19th century, prices were improving. Machines were invented to spin, weave and dye fabrics. They did the job faster than workers and were cheaper too.

Then, in 1845, an American, Elias Howe, invented sewing machines. Tailors were delighted. The machines saved them hours of hard work.

The next breakthrough was ready-made clothes. Normally ladies and gentlemen would tell their tailors what to make, but Charles Worth had a better idea. He created new dresses to his own designs, then invited rich ladies to come and buy them.

His wife, Marie, was the world's first fashion model. She dressed in her husband's latest outfits and paraded them around his shop.

Rich ladies

Charles Worth

Marie Worth

By the 1860s, Worth had a thousand people working for him... and his client list included nine queens. Other designers decided to copy and set up their own rival fashion houses.

For ordinary people, department stores were the answer. These stores sold cheap imitations of the fashion house designs. Most shoppers weren't bothered about brand names. They just wanted stylish clothes at an affordable price.

Chapter 8

The sporty look

For centuries, fashionable clothes were far from sensible. Even when women went riding or mountain climbing, they still had to dress in corsets, hoops and frills.

"Our clothes are uncomfortable and unhealthy," thought some radical women in America. Their solution was a jacket and a knee-length skirt, worn over very baggy trousers.

Amelia Bloomer

Amelia Bloomer journeyed to London and Dublin to promote this new outfit. But the trip was a disaster. A few brave women tried to copy her. Everyone else just laughed.

Thirty years later, bicycles were invented. Women and men rushed to ride them, but cycling in a skirt was never going to be easy. Baggy trousers (without the skirt) were the perfect solution. People named them *bloomers* after their creator.

Bloomers soon caught on for other sports too.

Swimwear also needed to improve. Since the 1700s, doctors had prescribed swimming in the sea for good health. But people were afraid of revealing too much flesh. For years men and women bathed in long, floaty shirts.

They even invented bathing machines – changing rooms on wheels, where shy swimmers could hide until they were safely out at sea.

As times changed, ladies were allowed to show their ankles, then their calves, and finally their knees.

1860s

1890s

1920s

Men tried swimming in long shorts, but they kept falling down. The all-in-one suit came to the rescue, followed by the belt. Then Lycra changed swimwear forever.

1880s

1930s

1960s

Chapter 9

Anything goes

The 20th century saw the most dramatic changes in fashion. When out walking, Edwardian ladies forced themselves into S-bend corsets, which made their bottoms and chests stick out.

For tea parties with friends, they changed into flowing gowns. These hung in graceful folds and were much more comfortable.

In the evenings they dressed up in closer-fitting gowns made of silk or satin and trimmed with lace. They backcombed their hair and piled it high on their head.

But after the First World War, women reacted against these feminine styles. They adopted a more boyish look, flattening their breasts, wearing unwaisted dresses and cutting their hair short. Leading the way were American dancers, known as flappers.

Meanwhile, well-to-do men wore a lounge suit during the day, and a black tail coat on evenings out. This three-piece suit was based on the one invented by Louis XIV. The major change was long trousers instead of knee-length hose.

Evening suit

Lounge suit

During the Second World War, there were strict rules on buying clothes and fabric. As a result, shorter, more practical fashions developed. Inspired by soldiers' uniforms, belts and square shoulders also became popular.

In the 1950s, fashion designers really went to town. Luxurious, extravagant designs made up for rationing during the war.

But clothes also became an expression of freedom. The 1960s saw some radical new ideas.

Designer Mary Quant introduced the mini skirt.

Pop groups popularized ethnic clothes from the East.

And daring new styles came from young people on the streets.

58

Today, anyone can spark off the latest fashion, from models on the catwalk...

...to kids after school.

Who knows what fashions tomorrow will bring?

What's in a name?

In 1818, a Scottish chemist, Charles Macintosh, invented a waterproof fabric. His early versions were very smelly, but the idea was popular. Soon any coats made from the fabric were known as **macintoshes**.

By the 1830s, every well-dressed lady wanted puffy sleeves. Their name – **gigot sleeves** – sounded foreign and fancy, but *gigot* is really French for leg of lamb.

60

James Thomas Brudenell was the seventh Earl of Cardigan and a British general. He's remembered today for the knitted wool jacket he loved to wear – the **cardigan**.

Dungaree is a coarse Indian fabric (*dungri* in Hindi). It was used to make a new style of workmen's overalls, soon to be named **dungarees**.

Hundreds of years ago, another coarse fabric was made in Nimes, France. The French for "from Nimes" is *de Nimes*. Now the same fabric is made all over the world... and it's known as **denim**.

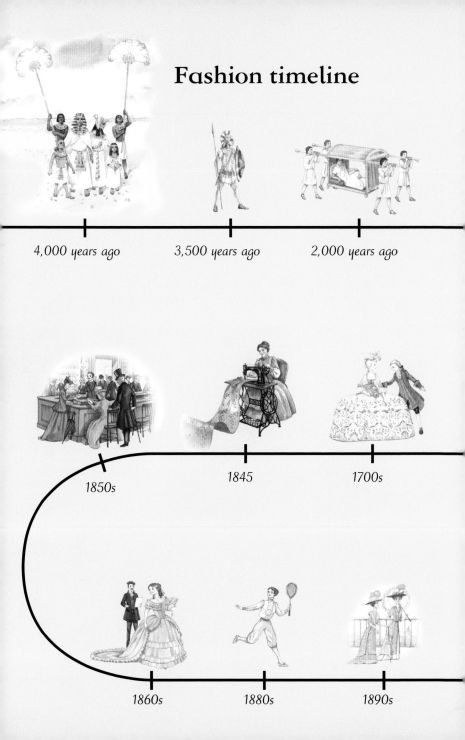

Fashion timeline

4,000 years ago

3,500 years ago

2,000 years ago

1850s

1845

1700s

1860s

1880s

1890s

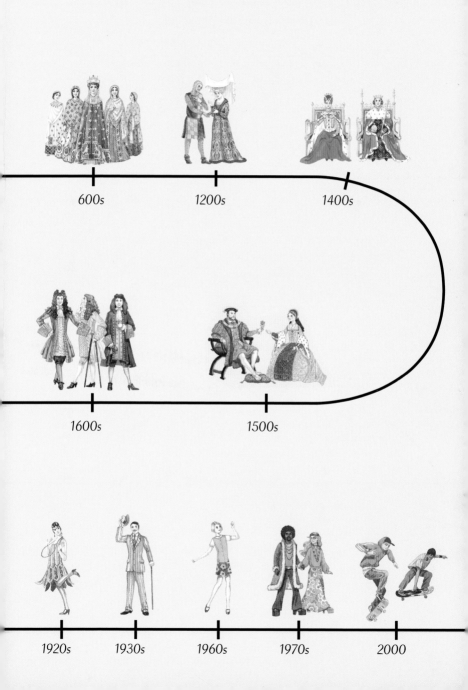

600s

1200s

1400s

1600s

1500s

1920s

1930s

1960s

1970s

2000

Series editor: Lesley Sims

Designed by Amanda Gulliver
and Mike Olley

Cover design by Russell Punter

First published in 2006 by Usborne Publishing Ltd., Usborne House,
83-85 Saffron Hill, London EC1N 8RT, England. www.usborne.com
Copyright © 2006 Usborne Publishing Ltd.

64